YOUR KNOWLEDGE HAS VALUE

Nicholas Liberto

Edgar Allen Poe, The Fall of the House of Usher. An Analysis

GRIN Verlag

Bibliografische Information der Deutschen Nationalbibliothek:

Die Deutsche Bibliothek verzeichnet diese Publikation in der Deutschen National-
bibliografie; detaillierte bibliografische Daten sind im Internet über http://dnb.d-
nb.de/ abrufbar.

Imprint:

Copyright © 2010 GRIN Verlag GmbH
Druck und Bindung: Books on Demand GmbH, Norderstedt Germany
ISBN: 978-3-656-54114-1

This book at GRIN:

http://www.grin.com/en/e-book/264864/edgar-allen-poe-the-fall-of-the-house-of-
usher-an-analysis

Edgar Allen Poe's short story, *The Fall of the House of Usher* relies heavily on symbolism and suspense to create a haunting atmosphere that leaves the reader on the edge of their seat. The story is rich with descriptions of both the setting and characters, and this story about the love turned lust of brother and sister comes to a tragic end in the traditional Poe style. Relying heavily on the then-new theories of Freud and Jung's psychoanalysis (Lawrence 1686), Poe creates a story where the dark and somber house of Usher is intertwined with its inhabitants, climaxing in the end by the house collapsing along with the remains of the family that once lived inside. *The Fall of the House of Usher* is at heart an extended metaphor; using the house to symbolize the decay and ultimate collapse of a bloodline tainted by incest. The Usher family, of whom only the infirm Roderick and recently 'deceased' Madeline remain, is inexorably tied with their dwelling, as they both perish and sink into the tarn surrounding the home. Great care is given to the description of the house and how it can be seen to relate to the Usher bloodline, specifically their "direct line of descent" (Poe 1116).

It is very clear upon the beginning of the short story that the un-named narrator can be none other than the protagonist. The reader cannot help but allow themselves to be drawn into the story through his observations of the Usher household. This narrator arrives at the home as the result of a summons he received from its owner, Roderick Usher. This letter contained "evidence of nervous agitation. The writer spoke of acute bodily illness-of a mental disorder that oppressed him-and of an earnest desire to see me, as his best, and indeed only personal friend" (Poe 1116). Dutifully, the narrator arrives at the Usher household in order to honor that request made on behalf of their once strong friendship. Upon arrival, the plot of the story begins its rising action, as the narrator begins to integrate himself into the Usher household and way of life. He is greeted for example not by his friend directly, but rather a frustrated family doctor, and then an un-named servant who leads him up "dark and intricate passageways to the studio of his master" (Poe 1117). The reader almost begins to tense up as the image of the narrator moving through a completely blackened house begins to take form, the atmosphere itself depicted as an "irredeemable gloom that hung over all" (Poe 1117), slowly driving the narrator deeper and deeper into paranoia and fear.

The rising action picks up at a fever pitch upon the integration of the narrator into the Usher household. Days of un-ending gloom and boredom pass in the house as the weak remains of Lady Madeline finally succumb to the genetic illness that baffled her physician, mentioned once upon the night of her passing, and only elaborated upon when Roderick adds that she is being temporarily interred in the house where she would not suffer the "'obtrusive and eager inquires on the part of the family medicine men." (Poe 1123). The narrator is even forced to participate in the burial of Lady Madeline into a room below his own sleeping quarters that had once served as a dungeon and later as a store room for gunpowder during feudal times. Roderick and the narrator share this grim task, and then immediately is forced to witness his friend throw open the windows and stand in the face of a fierce thunderstorm. The rising action continues as the storm is described as "a whirlwind...with winds careening from all points against each other, without passing away into the distance" (Poe 1124). Poe creates an atmosphere of madness from this point onwards in the novel, as the storm rages outside the narrator is forced to whether a mental storm internally as he struggles to calm the hysterics of his companion. In a moment of desperation, he selects a novel entitled *Mad Trist* by Sir Lancelot Canning, remembering it had been a favorite of Roderick's in the past. This only serves to heighten the mood of tension and insanity in the house as what the narrator reads seems to come to life. This is best exemplified when the passage about the champion slaying the mighty dragon is read, where the death roar of the beast becomes a "distinct, hollow, clangorous, and yet apparently muffled reverberation" (Poe 1126). Roderick flies into a fit of hysterics, utterly convinced his deceased sister has come back from the grave to take her brother-lover with her, culminating with his screaming of "Madman! I Tell

you now she stands upon the door!" (Poe 1127). True to his word, Lady Madeline stands at the door in

her funeral shroud, immediately falling upon her brother, dragging both of them to the floor, dead in

the story's terrifying climax. Aghast at what he has seen, the narrator flees from the chamber, and from

the house as the walls begins to crack and shake. A "blood red moon" is seen from a fissure in the ceiling

of the home, and finally the walls come down, leaving only a tarnished plaque with the words "HOUSE

OF USHER" emblazoned upon it.

It can be clearly seen through the plot that the house stands not just as the place in which

Roderick and Madeline physically live, but also as the symbolic barometer for the health of the family

bloodline. A house the size of the Usher's must have at one time been strong and powerfully built, and

indeed the narrator makes several references to the house once standing as a fortress in feudal times.

The decayed and dismal state of the current house he enters is but a pale comparison to what it must

have been, similar to the Usher family. What once was a powerful and wealthy family was now reduced

to decay, along with their home. Literary critics Cleanth Brooks and Robert Warren seem to corroborate

this view in their article *A New Critical Reading of "The Fall of the House of Usher"*. After a brief

description of the literary devices Poe employs to haunt his readers, they state that "Roderick Usher

impresses the reader as being thoroughly doomed as the decaying house in which he lives" (Brooks &

Penn 1691). There is a definite and concrete connection between the Usher family and their dwelling

that stretches further than their simultaneous deaths.

Works Cited:

1) Poe, Edgar Allen. *The Fall of the House of Usher*. Boston: Bedford, 2007. Print.

2) Lawrence, D.H. . *On "The Fall of the House of Usher*. Boston: Bedford, 1919. Print.

3) Brooks, Cleanth, and Robert Penn Warren. *A New Critical Reading of "The Fall of the House of Usher"*. Boston: Bedford, 1943. Print.